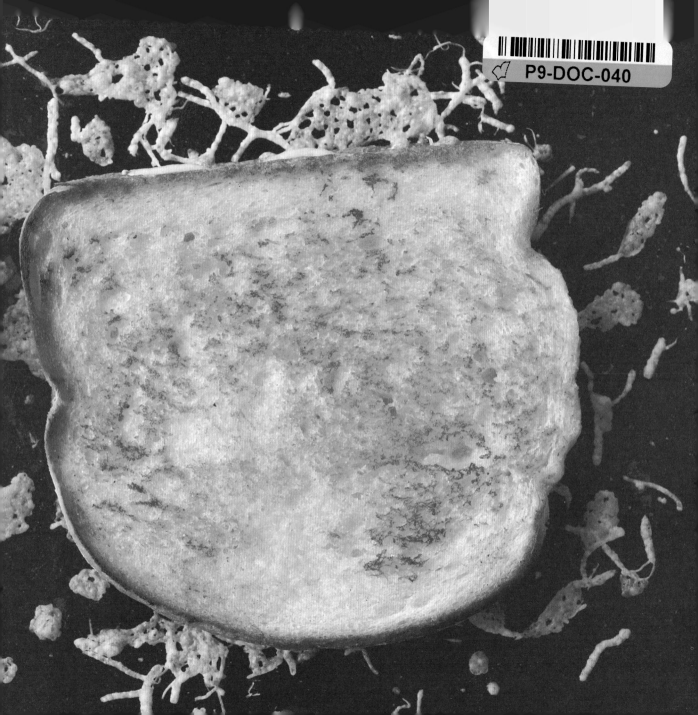

GRILLED CHEESE

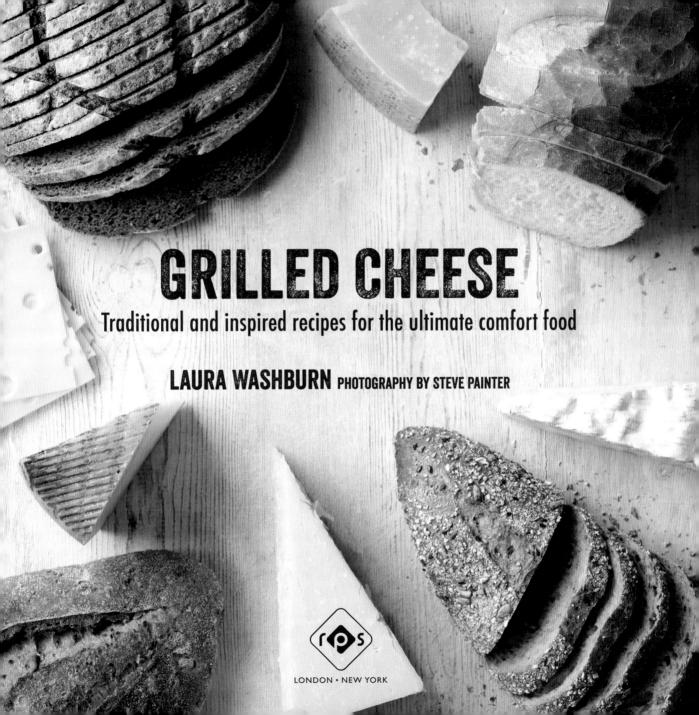

GRILLED CHEESE

Traditional and inspired recipes for the ultimate comfort food

LAURA WASHBURN PHOTOGRAPHY BY STEVE PAINTER

LONDON · NEW YORK

DESIGN, PHOTOGRAPHY AND PROP STYLING
Steve Painter
COMMISSIONING EDITOR Nathan Joyce
PRODUCTION CONTROLLER Meskerem Berhane
ART DIRECTOR Leslie Harrington
EDITORIAL DIRECTOR Julia Charles
FOOD STYLIST Lucy McKelvie

First published in 2014 by
Ryland Peters & Small
20–21 Jockey's Fields
London WC1R 4BW
and
519 Broadway, 5th Floor
New York, NY 10012
www.rylandpeters.com
10 9 8 7 6 5 4 3 2 1

Text © Laura Washburn 2014
Design and photographs
© Ryland Peters & Small 2014

ISBN: 978-1-84975-555-9

A CIP record for this book is available from
the British Library.

US Library of Congress cataloging-in-
Publication Data has been applied for

Printed in China

NOTES
* All spoon measurements are level, unless
otherwise specified
* All eggs are medium UK/large US, unless
otherwise specified. Recipes containing
raw or partially cooked egg should not be
served to the very young, very old, anyone
with a compromised immune system or
pregnant women.

ACKNOWLEDGEMENTS
Thanks to the team at RPS for doing such
a terrific job, again.

CONTENTS

06 INTRODUCTION
08 SIMPLE
24 GLOBAL
38 WICKED
50 GOURMET
64 INDEX

INTRODUCTION

THE GRILLED CHEESE SANDWICH IS ONE OF LIFE'S LITTLE PLEASURES. IT'S A SIMPLE THING, A COMFORTING THING, IT PLEASES CHILDREN AND ADULTS ALIKE. BUT DOES ANYONE ACTUALLY NEED A RECIPE FOR GRILLED CHEESE? AFTER ALL, IT IS JUST CHEESE AND BREAD WITH BUTTER, COOKED IN A PAN, RIGHT? HOW HARD CAN THAT BE? NOT HARD AT ALL IS THE TRUTH, BUT, GETTING THE RIGHT COMBINATION OF INGREDIENTS IS CRUCIAL IF YOU WANT TO ELEVATE A BASIC GRILLED CHEESE SANDWICH TO SOMETHING HEAVENLY. FOR STARTERS, THERE ARE SO MANY VARIABLES: WHICH KIND OF CHEESE, HOW THE CHEESE REACTS WHEN HEATED, WHICH TYPE OF BREAD, WHICH TYPE OF PAN AND WHAT TO COMBINE WITH THE CHEESE. THESE DETAILS LEAD TO THE ALL-IMPORTANT RESULT: A GRILLED CHEESE SANDWICH, MADE PROPERLY – CRISP AND GOLDEN BROWN ON THE OUTSIDE WITH A GOOEY MOLTEN INTERIOR. AS THIS DOES NOT JUST APPEAR ON THE PLATE WITHOUT SOME PLANNING AND SKILL, BELOW IS A GUIDE TO THE IMPORTANT ASPECTS OF THE ART OF THE GRILLED CHEESE SANDWICH.

GRILLED CHEESE BASICS

THE CHEESE... Contrary to popular belief, not all cheese melts well. Most cheeses melt, but some don't melt very well – the really fresh kind (very spreadable in consistency) or the dry, crumbly and aged cheeses, like Pecorino; every cheese in-between is good for a melted sandwich.

THE BREAD... Anything goes, really, provided it can be coated with a thin layer of room temperature butter. Thick slices of bread, or rolls, need to be pressed down. There are fancy presses for just such a thing, and these are useful when cooking more than one sandwich at a time. You can always use a spatula or a potato masher, though, to achieve pretty much the same result.

THE PAN... For an easy life, opt for as large as possible and non-stick. Cast iron works if it is well seasoned and has ridges. Whatever you choose, a thick base is important to conduct heat evenly. Also, use low-medium or medium – never high – or the bread will burn before the cheese melts.

THE EXTRAS... For everything else, you need a beautiful cookbook full of ideas and inspirations to get you started.

SIMPLE

BASIC GRILLED CHEESE

THIS IS THE BASIC GRILLED CHEESE METHOD, WHICH CAN BE USED AS A BLUEPRINT FOR ALL SORTS OF EXPERIMENTATION. FOR A MORE COMPLEX TASTE, IT'S A GOOD IDEA TO COMBINE TWO RELATIVELY MILD CHEESES, SUCH AS A MILD CHEDDAR AND MONTEREY JACK.

4 large slices white bread

Unsalted butter, softened

300 g/3¼ cups mixed grated/shredded mild cheeses, such as mild Cheddar, Gruyére, Monterey Jack or Gouda

SERVES 2

Butter each of the bread slices on one side and arrange them buttered-side down on a clean work surface or chopping board.

It's best to assemble the sandwiches in a large, non-stick frying pan/skillet before you heat it up. Start by putting two slices of bread in the frying pan/skillet, butter-side down. If you can only accommodate one slice in your pan, you'll need to cook one sandwich at a time. Top each slice with half of the grated/shredded cheese, but be careful not to let too much cheese fall into the pan. Top with the final pieces of bread, butter-side up.

Turn the heat to medium and cook for 3–4 minutes on the first side, then carefully turn with a large spatula and cook on the second side for 2–3 minutes until the sandwiches are golden brown all over and the cheese is visibly melted.

Remove from the frying pan/skillet and cut the sandwiches in half. Let cool for a few minutes before serving and dunk to your heart's content in a lovely steaming bowl of tomato soup.

RED ONION CHUTNEY & CHEDDAR

CHEDDAR AND CHUTNEY IS A WINNING COMBINATION BUT FOR BEST RESULTS, BE SURE TO USE A REALLY GUTSY MATURE/SHARP CHEDDAR HERE. THE CHUTNEY NEEDS TO HAVE A GOOD BALANCE OF SWEETNESS AND TARTNESS TO MAKE THIS WORK PERFECTLY, SO BE SURE TO TASTE AND ADJUST BEFORE ASSEMBLING THE SANDWICHES.

4 slices white bread

Unsalted butter, softened

150 g/1¾ cups grated/shredded mature/sharp Cheddar

FOR THE QUICK CHUTNEY

2 red onions, halved and thinly sliced

2 tablespoons vegetable oil

Good pinch of salt

1 tablespoon light brown sugar

2 tablespoons wine vinegar

2 tablespoons balsamic vinegar

SERVES 2

In a small non-stick frying pan/skillet, combine the onions and oil over a medium-high heat and cook, stirring occasionally, until caramelized. Add the remaining ingredients, reduce the heat to a simmer and cook until the mixture is sticky but still somewhat liquid. Taste and adjust the seasoning, adding more sugar for sweetness or vinegar for tartness, as required.

Butter each of the bread slices on one side and set aside.

Without turning the heat on, place two slices of bread in a large, ridged griddle/stovetop pan, butter-side down. If you can only fit one slice in your pan, you'll need to cook one sandwich at a time. Spread generously with some of the chutney and sprinkle each slice with half the grated/shredded cheese in an even layer. Cover each slice with another bread slice, butter-side up.

Turn the heat to medium and cook the first side for 3–4 minutes until it turns a deep golden colour, pressing gently with a spatula. Carefully turn with the spatula and cook on the second side for 2–3 minutes, or until deep golden brown all over. To achieve the lovely criss-cross pattern, turn the sandwiches over again, rotate them 90° to the left or right and cook for a final 2–3 minutes.

Remove from the frying pan/skillet, transfer to a plate and cut the sandwiches in half. Let cool for a few minutes before serving with extra chutney.

NOTE: Leftover chutney, if any, can be kept in the refrigerator in a sealed container.

THREE CHEESE

THIS IS MOST DEFINITELY NOT ROCKET SCIENCE, JUST CHEESE AND BUTTERED BREAD. WHAT ELEVATES IT ABOVE THE CROWD IS CAREFULLY CHOOSING THE RIGHT BLEND OF CHEESE: MOZZARELLA FOR ITS MELTING QUALITY, SOMETHING INTENSE LIKE A GOOD MATURE/SHARP CHEDDAR AND EMMENTAL/SWISS CHEESE FOR A HINT OF NUTTINESS. YUM!

70 g/scant 1 cup grated/shredded Lincolnshire Poacher or mature/sharp Cheddar

70 g/scant 1 cup grated/shredded Emmental/Swiss cheese

125 g/4½ oz. mozzarella, sliced

4 large slices white bread

Unsalted butter, softened

SERVES 2

Butter each of the bread slices on one side and set aside.

Without turning the heat on, place two slices of bread in a large, non-stick frying pan/skillet, butter-side down. If you can only accommodate one slice in your pan, you'll need to cook one sandwich at a time. Sprinkle the slices in the pan with half of the grated/shredded Lincolnshire Poacher or Cheddar in an even layer. Top with half of the mozzarella slices, then sprinkle half of the grated/shredded Emmental/Swiss cheese on top. Finally, enclose with the remaining bread slices, butter-side up.

Turn the heat to medium and cook the first side for 3–5 minutes until it turns a deep golden colour. Carefully turn with a spatula and cook on the second side for 2–3 minutes, or until deep golden brown all over.

Remove from the frying pan/skillet, transfer to a plate and cut the sandwiches into quarters. Let cool for a few minutes before serving. Dunk the quarters into a nice hot bowl of tomato soup.

BALSAMIC MUSHROOMS & FONTINA

TANGY BALSAMIC MUSHROOMS OFFER AN EARTHY FOIL TO THE RICHNESS OF THE MELTED FONTINA. LIKE MOST GRILLED CHEESE SANDWICHES, THIS ONE GOES WELL WITH TOMATO SOUP, BUT ALSO WORKS NICELY WITH A HEARTY CREAM OF MUSHROOM SOUP.

2 tablespoons unsalted butter

1 tablespoon vegetable oil

125 g/1⅔ cups white mushrooms, thinly sliced

1 shallot, diced

½ teaspoon dried thyme

Salt and freshly ground black pepper

3 tablespoons balsamic vinegar

1 teaspoon red wine vinegar

150g/2 cups grated/shredded Fontina, or use thin slices

4 slices granary/granary-style bread

Unsalted butter, softened

SERVES 2

In a non-stick frying pan/skillet, combine the butter, oil, mushrooms, shallot and thyme over a medium-high heat and cook, stirring occasionally, until everything is soft and deep golden in colour. Season well, add the vinegars and simmer until the liquid almost evaporates. Taste and adjust the seasoning.

Butter each of the bread slices on one side and set aside.

Without turning the heat on, place two slices of bread in a large, non-stick frying pan/skillet, butter-side down. If you can only fit one slice in your pan/skillet, you'll need to cook one sandwich at a time. Spoon over half of the mushrooms and sprinkle half of the grated/shredded cheese on top in an even layer. Cover each slice with another bread slice, butter-side up.

Turn the heat to medium and cook the first side for 3–5 minutes until it turns a deep golden colour, pressing gently with a spatula. Carefully turn with the spatula and cook on the second side for 2–3 minutes, or until deep golden brown all over.

Remove from the frying pan/skillet, transfer to a plate and cut the sandwiches in half. Let cool for a few minutes before serving alongside a hot bowl of mushroom soup.

LEEK & GRUYÈRE

I ALWAYS ASSOCIATE LEEKS WITH FRENCH CUISINE AND GRUYÈRE IS CERTAINLY UP THERE AMONG THE FINEST OF THE FRENCH CHEESES. IF A GRILLED CHEESE SANDWICH COULD BE FRENCH, IT WOULD BE THIS ONE – SIMPLE YET ELEGANT. SERVE WITH A GLASS OF CHILLED WHITE WINE FROM THE LOIRE VALLEY.

1 large leek, rinsed and sliced thinly into rounds

1 teaspoon vegetable oil

1 tablespoon unsalted butter

½ teaspoon dried thyme

Salt and freshly ground black pepper

6 tablespoons dry white wine

4 slices white bread

Unsalted butter, softened

Wholegrain Dijon mustard

250 g/2 cups grated/shredded Gruyére

SERVES 2

In a non-stick frying pan/skillet, combine the leek, oil, butter and thyme over a medium-high heat and cook, stirring occasionally, until soft and golden. Season well, add the wine and simmer until the liquid evaporates. Taste and adjust the seasoning. Set aside.

Butter each of the bread slices on one side, then spread two of the slices with mustard on the non-buttered side and set all the slices aside.

Without turning the heat on, place two slices of bread in a large, ridged griddle/stovetop pan, butter-side down. If you can only fit one slice in your pan, you'll need to cook one sandwich at a time. Spoon half of the leeks over each slice and sprinkle over half the grated/shredded cheese in an even layer. Cover with another bread slice each, mustard-side down.

Turn the heat to medium and cook the first side for 3–5 minutes until it turns a deep golden colour, pressing gently with a spatula. Carefully turn with the spatula and cook on the second side for 2–3 minutes, or until deep golden brown all over.

Remove from the ridged griddle/stovetop pan, transfer to a plate and cut the sandwiches in half. Let cool for a few minutes before serving.

VARIATION: Other good French cheeses to try here include Beaufort, Comté and Raclette.

MOZZARELLA PUTTANESCA

HALFWAY BETWEEN A PIZZA AND A PASTA SAUCE, THIS SANDWICH BRINGS TOGETHER CLASSIC ITALIAN INGREDIENTS. GOOD QUALITY CHEESES MAKE ALL THE DIFFERENCE, SO BE SURE TO USE THE REAL THING AND YOU'LL BE IN FOR A TREAT.

Large round or square focaccia, halved lengthways and widthways

Extra virgin olive oil

4 tablespoons black olive paste

2 tablespoons sun-dried tomato paste

4–6 tablespoons passata/strained tomatoes

2 mozzarella balls, drained and thinly sliced

2 teaspoons dried oregano

2 tablespoons grated/shredded Parmesan

2–3 tablespoons capers, drained

Good pinch of chilli/hot red pepper flakes

Few fresh basil leaves, torn

SERVES 2–4

Brush the outsides of the focaccia halves with olive oil and arrange oil-side down on a clean work surface or chopping board.

Spread two of the non-oiled sides generously with the olive paste. Spread the other two non-oiled sides with the sun-dried tomato paste, then top with the passata/strained tomatoes. Divide the mozzarella slices between the tomato-coated sides. Sprinkle over the oregano, Parmesan, capers and chilli/hot red pepper flakes. Scatter over a few basil leaves. Top with the olive oil-coated bread, oil-side up.

Without turning the heat on, place the two sandwiches in a large, non-stick frying pan/skillet. If you can only fit one sandwich in your pan/skillet, you'll need to cook one sandwich at a time.

Turn the heat to medium and cook the first side for 4–5 minutes, then carefully turn with a large spatula and cook the other side for 2–3 minutes, pressing down gently with the spatula until golden brown all over.

Remove from the frying pan/skillet, transfer to a wooden chopping board or a plate and cut the sandwiches in half. Let cool for a few minutes before serving.

KIMCHI & MONTEREY JACK

MELTED CHEESE REALLY BENEFITS FROM SOMETHING SOUR OR TANGY TO ACT AS A FOIL FOR THE RICHNESS. HERE, KIMCHI, A SPICED KOREAN CONDIMENT OF FERMENTED PICKLED CABBAGE, DOES JUST THAT TO PERFECTION. THE COMBINATION MAY SOUND STRANGE AT FIRST, BUT IT REALLY IS FANTASTIC. TO BEST ENJOY THE CONTRASTING TASTES AND TEXTURES, USE PLAIN WHITE BREAD WITH THE CRUSTS TRIMMED.

60 g/½ cup kimchi

150 g/1¾ cups grated/shredded mild cheese, such as Monterey Jack or mild Cheddar

4 slices white bread, crusts removed

Unsalted butter, softened

SERVES 2

First remove the crusts from the 4 slices of bread. Butter each of the bread slices on one side and set aside.

Pat the kimchi dry with paper towels to remove excess moisture and chop.

Without turning the heat on, put two slices of bread in a large, heavy-based non-stick frying pan/skillet, butter-side down. If two slices won't fit, cook them in batches. Top with half the kimchi and sprinkle over half the grated/shredded cheese in an even layer. Cover with another bread slice, butter-side up.

Turn the heat to medium and cook the first side for 3–5 minutes until it turns a deep golden colour, pressing gently with a spatula. Carefully turn with the spatula and cook on the second side for 2–3 minutes, or until deep golden brown all over.

Remove from the frying pan/skillet, transfer to a plate and cut in half. Let cool for a few minutes before serving. Repeat for the remaining sandwich if necessary.

NOTE: Vegetarians should note that kimchi often contains fish as part of the seasoning.

BRIE & APPLE-CRANBERRY SAUCE

WALNUTS GO BRILLIANTLY WITH BRIE AND CRANBERRIES, AS DO MOST OTHER NUTS, SO FEEL FREE TO SUBSTITUTE SOMETHING ELSE IF WALNUT BREAD IS NOT AVAILABLE. A TIP FOR PREPARATION: THIN SLICES OF BRIE MELT MORE SUCCESSFULLY SO BE SURE TO KEEP THE CHEESE WELL CHILLED, WHICH MAKES IT EASIER TO SLICE. ALSO, REMOVE THE RIND BECAUSE IT DOES NOT MELT WELL.

About 180g/6 oz. ripe chilled Brie, rind removed, sliced thinly or finely diced

4–8 slices walnut bread, depending on size of loaf

Unsalted butter, softened

FOR THE APPLE-CRANBERRY SAUCE

300 g/3 cups cranberries, fresh or frozen

Juice of 1 orange

1 small tart cooking apple, such as Cox, peeled and diced

About 3 tablespoons caster/granulated sugar or more to taste

SERVES 2

For the apple-cranberry sauce, combine all the ingredients in a saucepan over a low heat. Stir the mixture often, until the sugar dissolves and the cranberries begin to pop and disintegrate. If the mixture is too dry, add a small amount of water. Cover and simmer gently until the cranberries are tender and the mixture has a jam-like consistency; keep checking to see if the mixture is too dry – if it is, add water bit-by-bit to prevent the mixture from thickening and burning. Taste and adjust sweetness to your liking. Set aside until needed.

Butter the bread slices on one side and set aside.

This is easiest if assembled in the pan. Without turning the heat on, place two slices of bread in a large, heavy-based non-stick frying pan/skillet, butter-side down. If you can't fit two slices side-by-side in the pan/skillet, you'll need to cook them in two batches. Spread the slices generously with some of the cranberry sauce, then top with brie slices. Cover with the remaining bread slices, butter-side up.

Turn the heat to medium and cook the first side for 3–5 minutes until it turns a deep golden colour, pressing gently with a spatula. Carefully turn with the spatula and cook on the second side for 2–3 minutes, or until deep golden brown all over.

Remove from the frying pan/skillet, transfer to a plate and cut in half. Let cool for a few minutes before serving along with extra apple-cranberry sauce.

NOTE: Leftover cranberry sauce can be kept in the refrigerator in a sealed container.

GLOBAL

WELSH RAREBIT

AN EXQUISITE VEHICLE FOR SOME WONDERFUL, TYPICALLY BRITISH INGREDIENTS: INTENSE CHEDDAR, TANGY WORCESTERSHIRE SAUCE AND MELLOW MUSTARD POWDER, ALL BOUND TOGETHER WITH THE BITTERNESS OF ALE. INCREDIBLY SIMPLE AND DEEPLY SATISFYING, YOU CAN SERVE THIS ANY TIME OF DAY OR NIGHT.

4 slices ciabatta or sourdough bread

30 g/2 tablespoons unsalted butter, plus extra for spreading

30 g/3 tablespoons plain/all-purpose flour

125 ml/½ cup ale, at room temperature

1 teaspoon mustard powder

150 g/1½ cups mature/sharp Cheddar, grated/shredded

1 tablespoon Worcestershire sauce

Pinch of ground cayenne pepper

SERVES 2

Butter each of the bread slices on one side and arrange them buttered-side down on a clean work surface or chopping board.

In a small saucepan over a low heat, combine the butter and flour, stirring until melted. Pour the ale in gradually and stir continuously until the mixture thickens. Add the mustard powder, cheese, Worcestershire sauce and cayenne pepper and stir to just melt the cheese before taking the pan off the heat.

Put two slices of bread in a large frying pan/skillet, butter-side down. If you can't fit two pieces of bread in the pan/skillet, cook them one at a time. Top each slice with half of the cheese, then enclose with the other slices of bread, buttered-side up.

Turn the heat to medium and cook for 3–4 minutes on the first side, then carefully turn with a large spatula and cook on the other side for 1–2 minutes more until golden brown all over.

Remove from the pan/skillet and cut in half. Let cool for a few minutes before serving.

MONTE CRISTO

THIS IS A CLASSIC AMERICAN DINER SANDWICH AND ONE I LOVED AS CHILD. IT IS BASICALLY FRENCH TOAST STUFFED WITH HAM AND OOZING MELTED CHEESE, SERVED WITH JAM FOR SPREADING OR DIPPING INTO. SOME VERSIONS USE SLICED TURKEY AS WELL, WHICH IS JUST AS AUTHENTIC. VERY RETRO, AND A SEEMINGLY STRANGE COMBINATION OF SWEET AND SAVOURY, THIS SANDWICH IS DELIGHTFUL. TRY IT AND SEE.

2 UK large/US extra large eggs

4 tablespoons milk

4 slices white bread

Unsalted butter, softened

4 slices or 250 g/scant 3 cups grated/shredded Emmental/Swiss cheese

2 slices ham, smoked or ordinary

Icing/confectioners' sugar, to dust

Strawberry jam/jelly, to serve

SERVES 2

In a shallow dish, use a balloon whisk to beat together the eggs and milk. Set aside.

Lay two pieces of bread down on a clean work surface or chopping board and top them with one slice of cheese each, followed by a slice of ham and finally another slice of cheese. Top with the remaining bread slices to enclose both sandwiches.

Gently melt a large knob/pat of butter in a non-stick frying pan/skillet.

Meanwhile, working one at a time, carefully dip the sandwiches in the beaten egg mixture, turning to coat both sides.

Transfer the sandwiches to the hot frying pan/skillet and cook the first side for 3–5 minutes until deep golden. Depending on the size of your pan/skillet, you may need to cook one sandwich at a time. Carefully turn with a large spatula and cook on the second side, for 2–3 minutes more or until golden brown all over.

Remove from the pan/skillet and transfer to a plate. Let cool for a few minutes, then dust with icing/confectioners' sugar, cut in half and serve with a little strawberry jam/jelly.

CHORIZO, MINI PEPPERS & MANCHEGO

THIS DECIDEDLY SPANISH-INSPIRED TREAT FEATURES A MAGICAL COMBINATION OF SPICY, SMOKY CHORIZO, SWEET MINI PEPPERS AND CREAMY MANCHEGO. IF YOU WANT A LITTLE EXTRA OOZINESS, REPLACE SOME OF THE MANCHEGO WITH MOZZARELLA. IF YOU'RE A SPICE FAN, WHY NOT SUBSTITUTE THE SWEET PEPPERS FOR PADRÓN PEPPERS FOR AN EXTRA KICK.

1–2 tablespoons extra virgin olive oil

100 g/3½ oz. mini (bell) peppers or padrón peppers

Salt

Unsalted butter, softened

4 slices sourdough or other artisan bread

100 g/3½ oz. chorizo, thinly sliced

250 g/3 cups grated/shredded Manchego

SERVES 2

Heat the oil in a small frying pan/skillet and add the peppers. Cook over a medium heat until charred all over, 5–10 minutes. Season lightly with salt and set aside.

Butter the bread slices on one side and arrange buttered-side down on a clean work surface or chopping board.

Divide the chorizo in half and arrange on two slices of bread. Next, divide the cheese in half and sprinkle two-thirds of each on top. Top with three or four peppers, then the remaining cheese. Enclose with the remaining bread, buttered-side up.

Place the two sandwiches in a large, heavy-based non-stick frying pan/skillet. Depending on the size of your pan/skillet, you may need to cook one sandwich at a time.

Turn the heat to medium and cook for 3–4 minutes on the first side. Carefully turn with a large spatula and cook on the second side, for 2–3 minutes more, pressing down gently on this side until golden brown all over.

Remove from the pan/skillet and cut in half. Let cool for a few minutes before serving.

HALLOUMI, FALAFEL & BEETROOT WITH TAHINI SAUCE

HALLOUMI IS A VERY SALTY CYPRIOT CHEESE WHICH TAKES WELL TO GRILLING OR FRYING IN A GRIDDLE PAN. AN UNUSUAL GRILLED CHEESE COMBO, THE TASTE WILL TRANSPORT YOU TO A MEDITERRANEAN ISLAND. NOT BAD FOR JUST A SANDWICH.

200 g/7 oz. halloumi, sliced

2 cooked beet(root), thinly sliced (about 125 g/4½ oz.)

6–8 falafel (about 125 g/4½ oz.), warmed

Extra virgin olive oil

4 flatbreads

FOR THE TAHINI SAUCE

½ cup tahini

Juice of ½ lemon

Salt and freshly ground black pepper

SERVES 2

For the sauce, combine the tahini and lemon juice and just enough water to obtain a nice dipping sauce consistency. Taste and adjust adding the seasoning and more lemon juice as required. Set aside.

Heat a ridged griddle/stovetop pan and fry the halloumi slices on both sides to form grill marks on the cheese. Remove and set aside.

Brush the outsides of the flatbreads with the oil and arrange oil-side down on a clean work surface or chopping board. For each sandwich, arrange the grilled halloumi slices, beet(root) and falafel, gently smushed over half the bread, then fold over the remaining bread to enclose the filling.

Place the sandwiches in the ridged griddle/stovetop pan. Depending on the size of your pan, you may need to cook one sandwich at a time.

Turn the heat to medium and cook 3–4 minutes on the first side. Carefully turn with a large spatula and cook on the second side, for 2–3 minutes more, pressing down gently on this side until golden brown all over.

Remove from the griddle pan and cut in half. Let cool for a few minutes before serving, with the tahini sauce for dipping and a couple of lemon wedges.

AVOCADO, REFRIED BEAN & MONTEREY JACK

THIS SANDWICH IS GREAT ANY TIME OF DAY, EITHER AS IT IS OR WITH A FRIED EGG ON TOP. FOR EXTRA HEAT, USE SPICY REFRIED BEANS. ANY KIND OF SALSA WILL GO NICELY ON THE SIDE.

150 g/2 cups grated/shredded Monterey Jack or mild Cheddar

200 g/scant cup refried beans

1 ripe avocado, sliced

4 slices white bread

Unsalted butter, softened

FOR THE SALSA

2 tomatoes, finely chopped

1 small red (bell) pepper, roughly chopped

2 spring onions/scallions, finely chopped

1 green chilli/chile pepper, finely chopped

Small bunch of coriander/cilantro, finely chopped

Freshly squeezed juice of 1 lime

Pinch of salt

SERVES 2

Butter the bread slices on one side and arrange buttered-side down on a clean work surface or chopping board. Spread the beans on the non-buttered side.

This is easiest if assembled in a large, non-stick frying pan/skillet. Put two slices of bread in the pan/skillet, butter-side down. If you can only fit one slice in your pan/skillet, you'll need to cook one sandwich at a time. Arrange half the avocado slices on top of each slice of bread, then sprinkle over half the grated cheese in an even layer. Cover with another bread slice, butter-side up.

Turn the heat to medium and cook the first side for 3–5 minutes until deep golden, pressing gently with a spatula. Carefully turn with a large spatula and cook on the second side, for 2–3 minutes more or until deep golden brown all over.

Meanwhile, make the salsa by combining all the ingredients and mixing thoroughly.

Remove the sandwiches from the pan/skillet, transfer to a plate and cut in half. Let them cool for a few minutes before serving with the salsa.

TANDOORI CHICKEN & MANGO CHUTNEY WITH PANEER

THE TASTE OF THIS SANDWICH DEPENDS ENTIRELY ON THE MANGO CHUTNEY SO USE THE BEST ONE YOU CAN FIND. SOMETHING WITH A BIT OF GINGER AND APPLE, ALTHOUGH LESS TRADITIONAL, PARTNERS THE MELTED CHEESE AMAZINGLY WELL. A SPOONFUL OF APPLE SAUCE CAN BE ADDED TO ORDINARY CHUTNEY IF DESIRED. SOME RAITA, IN A SMALL DISH, IS DELIGHTFUL FOR DIPPING.

2 boneless skinless chicken breasts (about 300 g/10 oz.)

4–5 tablespoons tandoori paste

Salt

2 thin slices mild cheese, such as Gouda or Fontina

100 g/scant cup grated/shredded paneer

4–6 tablespoons mango chutney, plus extra to serve

2 large naan breads

Unsalted butter, softened

FOR THE RAITA

250 ml/8 fl. oz. plain yogurt

½ cucumber, finely chopped

handful fresh mint, chopped

large pinch salt

SERVES 2

Heat the oven to 180°C (350°F) Gas 4. Coat the chicken liberally with the tandoori paste, season lightly with salt and bake until cooked through, 20–25 minutes. Let cool then slice thinly.

While the chicken is cooking, prepare the raita dip, by squeezing any excess moisture from the cucumber with paper towels and then mixing together all of the ingredients thoroughly. Set aside.

Butter the naan breads on one side and set aside.

This is easiest if assembled in a large heavy-based non-stick frying pan/skillet. You'll need to cook the sandwiches in two batches, as naan breads are fairly large. Put one slice of bread in the pan/skillet, butter-side down. You will need to fold the bread over to form a sandwich, so position the filling on one side. Put one slice of cheese on the naan, then arrange half the chicken slices over the top. Drop spoonfuls of the chutney on top then spread the spoonfuls out, gently and evenly. Sprinkle with half of the paneer. Fold one half of the bread over the top of the other half to cover.

Turn the heat to medium and cook the first side for 3–5 minutes until deep golden, pressing gently with a spatula. Carefully turn with a large spatula and cook on the second side, for 2–3 minutes more or until deep golden brown all over.

Remove from the pan/skillet and transfer to a plate. Let cool for a few minutes before serving. Repeat the cooking instructions for the remaining sandwich if necessary.

CHIPOTLE CHICKEN, ROASTED GREEN PEPPERS & QUESO FRESCO

IF POBLANO PEPPERS ARE AVAILABLE, USE THEM HERE INSTEAD OF THE GREEN (BELL) PEPPERS FOR A MORE AUTHENTIC TOUCH OF SOUTHWESTERN SPICE.

2 tablespoons vegetable oil

1 chipotle chilli/chile in adobo sauce, plus 1 teaspoon sauce, finely chopped

Juice of 1 lime

2 boneless skinless chicken breasts (about 300 g/10 oz.)

Pinch of salt

1 green (bell) pepper, cored and thinly sliced

1 round brown loaf, cut in half widthways and lengthways to form 4 triangular slices

Unsalted butter, softened

2 thin slices mild cheese, such as Gouda or Fontina

100 g/¾ cup crumbled queso fresco or feta

Small handful fresh coriander/cilantro, finely chopped

SERVES 2

Heat the oven to 180°C (350°F) Gas 4. In a small bowl, combine 1 tablespoon of the vegetable oil with the chilli/chile and lime juice and mix well. Coat the chicken breasts with this mixture, season with salt and bake until cooked through, 20–25 minutes. Let cool, then slice thinly.

Meanwhile, combine the remaining oil and (bell) pepper strips in a small non-stick frying pan/skillet and cook until softened and lightly charred. Set aside.

Butter all the bread slices on one side and set aside.

This is easiest if assembled in a large non-stick frying pan/skillet. Unless, you have a really large pan/skillet, you'll need to cook these sandwiches in batches. Put one slice of bread in the pan/skillet, butter-side down. Put one slice of cheese on top, then spread half of the chicken slices on top of the cheese. Arrange half the pepper strips on top and sprinkle with half of the crumbled cheese and coriander/cilantro. Cover with another bread slice, butter side up.

Turn the heat to medium and cook the first side for 4–5 minutes until deep golden, pressing gently with a spatula. Carefully turn with a large spatula and cook on the second side, for 2–3 minutes more or until deep golden brown all over.

Remove from the pan/skillet, transfer to a plate and let cool for a few minutes before serving. Repeat for the remaining sandwich.

WICKED

FRANKFURTER, SAUERKRAUT & MUSTARD

THE TASTE OF THIS SANDWICH RELIES HEAVILY ON THE QUALITY OF THE INGREDIENTS SO DO NOT SKIMP, ESPECIALLY WITH THE FRANKFURTERS. IF USING DARK BREAD, IT CAN BE DIFFICULT TO TELL WHEN IT IS BROWNING SO BE SURE NOT TO RUSH AND RAISE THE HEAT TO SPEED THE COOKING. IF IN DOUBT, USE YOUR NOSE. IF IT SMELLS DONE, IT PROBABLY IS!

4 very large slices pumpernickel or seeded rye bread

Unsalted butter, softened

2–3 tablespoons wholegrain Dijon mustard

4 large frankfurters, cooked and sliced in half widthways

100 g/1 cup sauerkraut or pickled cabbage, squeezed to remove excess moisture

250 g/3 cups mixed grated/shredded mild cheese, such as a combination of Emmental/Swiss and mild Cheddar

SERVES 2

Butter the bread slices on one side and arrange buttered side down on a clean work surface or chopping board. Spread two of the non-buttered sides generously with the mustard.

Assemble just before cooking, in a large, heavy-based frying pan/skillet. Depending on the size of your pan, you may need to cook one sandwich at a time.

Put the mustard-coated bread slices in the pan/skillet, butter-side down. Top each slice with half of the cheese, taking care not to let too much fall into the pan/skillet. Top this with half the frankfurter slices and follow with half the sauerkraut, arranging in an even layer. Top with the final piece of bread, butter-side up.

Turn the heat to medium and cook the first side for 3–4 minutes until deep golden, pressing gently with a spatula. Carefully turn with a large spatula and cook on the other side, for 2–3 minutes more or until deep golden brown all over.

Remove from the pan/skillet and let cool for a few minutes before serving. Repeat for the remaining sandwich, if necessary.

BURGER SCAMORZA

SCAMORZA IS AN ITALIAN SMOKED CHEESE, SIMILAR TO MOZZARELLA IN THAT IT HAS THE SAME BEAUTIFUL MELTING QUALITY, BUT WITH A LITTLE MORE PUNCH. THE BURGER FOR THIS SANDWICH NEEDS TO BE THIN-ISH FOR EASE OF COOKING AND EATING, SO IT IS FEASIBLE TO ALLOW TWO PER PERSON IF APPETITES ARE HEARTY. SERVE WITH FRIES, NATURALLY.

250 g/9 oz. minced/ground beef

1 small onion, grated

½ teaspoon garlic powder

½ teaspoon salt

Freshly ground black pepper

Dash of Worcestershire sauce, optional

2 white burger buns

Vegetable oil

300 g/10½ oz. scamorza or mozzarella, sliced

Tomato ketchup, for serving

gherkin/pickle spears, for serving

SERVES 2

In a mixing bowl, combine the minced/ground beef, onion, garlic powder, salt, pepper and Worcestershire sauce, if using, and mix well. Shape into two thin patties.

Slice the burger buns in half widthways. Brush the bun halves lightly on the outside with vegetable oil.

Heat up some vegetable oil in a large, heavy-based non-stick frying pan/skillet over a medium heat. When the pan/skillet is hot, cook the burgers for 3–5 minutes on each side, depending on how well-done you like your meat. Transfer the cooked burgers to a plate and set aside.

Clean the frying pan/skillet. If space allows, place two slices of bread, oil-side down in the pan/skillet (without turning the heat on), but you may have to cook them one at a time if they won't fit in the pan/skillet. Top each slice with one-quarter of the scamorza or mozzarella slices, then carefully place the burger on top. Follow this with another quarter of the cheese, so that the meat is nicely surrounded by cheese. Finally, cover with another bread slice, oil-side up.

Turn the heat to medium and cook the first side for 3–5 minutes until deep golden, pressing gently with a spatula. Carefully turn with a large spatula and cook on the other side, for 2–3 minutes more or until deep golden brown all over.

Let cool for a few minutes before serving. Repeat for the remaining sandwich if necessary.

VARIATION: Add two crispy, cooked streaky/American bacon rashers/slices per sandwich.

MEATBALLS, GARLIC TOMATO SAUCE & FONTINA

THIS FANTASTIC MELTING CHEESE OOZES AROUND THE SPHERES OF SEASONED BEEF TO PERFECTION.

1 large ciabatta, cut into 3 thick slices then cut widthways

4–6 slices or about 250 g/3 cups grated/shredded Fontina

FOR THE MEATBALLS

225 g/8 oz. minced/ground meat, half beef and half Italian sausage (see Note)

30 g/⅛ cup fresh breadcrumbs

1 teaspoon dried oregano

1 teaspoon dried rosemary

Pinch of chilli/hot red pepper flakes, or more to taste

1 egg, beaten

2 tablespoons milk, or more if necessary

1 teaspoon salt

Freshly ground black pepper

FOR THE GARLIC TOMATO SAUCE

3 garlic cloves, crushed but not peeled

Extra virgin olive oil

200 g/7 oz. passata/strained tomatoes

1 tablespoon unsalted butter

Pinch of caster/granulated sugar

Salt and ground black pepper

SERVES 2

Preheat the oven to 190°C (375°F) Gas 5. Line a baking sheet with parchment paper.

In a mixing bowl, combine all the meatball ingredients and mix well. The mixture should be firm enough to form into balls and moist enough so they are not dry; add more milk as required. Form them into 8–10 golf ball-sized balls and arrange on the baking sheet. Bake until browned and cooked though, 20–30 minutes. Remove from the oven and let cool slightly. Slice in half and set aside until needed.

Meanwhile, prepare the sauce. Coat the garlic cloves lightly with oil, place in a small ovenproof dish such as a ramekin and roast, at the same time as the meatballs, for 10–15 minutes, until golden and tender. Be careful not to let the garlic burn. Remove the garlic from the oven, slip the cloves from their skins and chop finely. In a small saucepan, melt the butter. Add the passata/strained tomatoes, garlic, sugar and salt and pepper. Simmer for 15 minutes. Taste and adjust seasoning. Keep warm until needed.

Coat the outsides of the bread slices with oil. It's best to assemble the sandwiches just before cooking, in a large, heavy-based non-stick frying pan/skillet. Depending on the size of your pan/skillet, you may need to cook them in batches. If space allows, put the three slices of bread, oil-side down, in the pan/skillet. Arrange half the cheese slices on top of each slice, then top with the meatball halves, dividing the pieces evenly between the two sandwiches. Coat the inside of the remaining bread pieces generously with the tomato sauce and place on top of the sandwich to enclose, oil-side up.

Turn the heat to medium and cook the first side for 3–4 minutes until deep golden, pressing gently with a spatula. Very carefully turn with a large spatula and cook on the other side, for 2–3 minutes more or until deep golden brown all over. Remove from the pan/skillet and let cool for a few minutes before serving. If the sandwich isn't holding together well, insert a small wooden skewer through the middle.

Note: If you can't buy Italian sausage, use half minced/ground beef and half minced/ground pork. Crush one teaspoon of fennel seeds using a pestle and mortar and add to the meat.

BBQ HAM HOCK & MAC 'N' CHEESE

YOU CAN NEVER HAVE TOO MUCH CHEESE IN A GRILLED CHEESE SANDWICH BUT HOW TO GET IT ALL IN IS THE DILEMMA. THE SOLUTION IS TO SNEAK IT IN ON THE BACK OF SOMETHING ELSE, LIKE MAC 'N' CHEESE. THIS RECIPE IS NOT FOR THE HEALTH CONSCIOUS BUT HOW MUCH HARM CAN JUST ONE SANDWICH DO? IT'S BEST MADE WITH LEFTOVER MAC 'N' CHEESE WHICH IS NOT TOO RUNNY.

4 slices wholemeal/whole-wheat sourdough bread

Unsalted butter, softened

180 g/6½ oz. cooked shredded ham hock

3–4 tablespoons spicy barbecue sauce, or to taste

2–4 big spoonfuls mac 'n' cheese

1–2 tablespoons sliced pickled jalapeños, optional

160 g/2 cups grated/shredded cheese, such as Cheddar or Monterey Jack

SERVES 2

Spread softened butter on the bread slices on one side. In a small saucepan, combine the ham and barbecue sauce and cook over a low heat, stirring, until warmed through. Set aside.

This is easiest if assembled in a large, heavy-based non-stick frying pan/skillet. Put one slice of bread in the pan/skillet, butter-side down. Top each bread slice with half of the cheese and half of the ham. It is best to drop the ham in spoonfuls and then spread the blobs out to the edges, gently, without disturbing the cheese beneath too much. Add jalapeños if using. Top this with blobs of mac 'n' cheese and spread gently to cover. Finally, top with a bread slice, butter-side up.

Turn the heat to medium and cook the first side for 5 minutes until deep golden, pressing gently with a spatula. Carefully turn with a large spatula and cook on the other side, for 2–3 minutes more or until deep golden brown all over.

Remove from the pan, transfer to a plate and cut in half. Let cool for a few minutes before serving. Repeat for the remaining sandwich if necessary.

CHILLI BACON SWISS CHEESE

THIS RECIPE INCLUDES A VERY QUICK, CHEAT'S CHILLI CON CARNE, WHICH IS PRETTY PERFECT, BUT IF YOU HAVE SOME LEFTOVER CHILLI CON CARNE, THIS SANDWICH WILL PUT IT TO GOOD USE. FOR THE CHEESE, ANY NUTTY-TASTING ALPINE CHEESE WORKS WELL HERE, OR EVEN A DUTCH CHEESE, BUT NOTHING TOO STRONG AS IT WILL BE OVERPOWERED BY THE SPICY MEAT.

FOR THE QUICK CHILLI CON CARNE

1 small onion, finely chopped

1 tablespoon vegetable oil

150 g/5½ oz. minced/ground beef

1 teaspoon dried oregano

1 tablespoon ground cumin

½ teaspoon chilli/hot red pepper flakes, or more to taste

½ teaspoon ground cayenne pepper, or more to taste

Salt and freshly ground black pepper

200 g/7 oz. passata/strained tomatoes

400-g/14-oz. can black beans, drained

6 rashers/slices streaky/American bacon

4 slices bread

Unsalted butter, softened

2–4 slices or 150 g/2 cups grated/shredded Emmental/Swiss cheese

SERVES 2

For the chilli con carne, combine the onion and oil in a frying pan/skillet over a medium heat and cook until soft and golden. Add the beef, herbs and spices and salt and pepper and cook, stirring occasionally, until browned. Add the passata/strained tomatoes and beans and simmer gently for at least 15 minutes. The mixture should be thick but not too thick; add a splash of water if necessary. Taste and adjust the seasoning.

Meanwhile, fry the bacon until crispy. Pat dry on paper towels and set aside.

Spread softened butter on the bread slices on one side.

This is easiest if assembled in a large heavy-based non-stick frying pan/skillet. Depending on the size of your pan, you may need to cook one sandwich at a time. If space allows, put two slices of bread in the pan/skillet, butter-side down. Top each slice with half of the cheese, half of the bacon and half of the chilli con carne. It is best to drop the chilli con carne in spoonfuls and then spread the blobs out to the edges, gently, without disturbing the cheese beneath too much. Enclose with the two remaining bread slices, butter-side up.

Turn the heat to medium and cook the first side for 3–5 minutes until deep golden, pressing gently with a spatula. Carefully turn with a large spatula and cook on the other side, for 2–3 minutes more or until deep golden brown all over.

Remove from the pan, transfer to a plate and cut in half. Let cool for a few minutes before serving. Repeat for the remaining sandwich if necessary.

PHILLY CHEESE STEAK SANDWICH

THE AUTHENTIC VERSION OF THIS SANDWICH CALLS FOR MELTED CHEESE TO TOP THE MEAT AND ONIONS, SO GRILLING IT IS A DEPARTURE FROM TRADITION. THE CHEESE CAN EITHER BE SWISS CHEESE OR PROCESSED CHEESE, BUT THIS RECIPE USES BOTH. THE DILL PICKLE IS NOT PART OF THE REAL THING, BUT IT ADDS A WELCOME TANG AND CRUNCH TO THIS SUBSTANTIAL CLASSIC.

2 large onions, thinly sliced

Unsalted butter and vegetable oil

Salt and freshly ground black pepper

350 g/12½ oz. minute/cube steak, thinly sliced

1 ciabatta or 2 long white rolls

3 tablespoons spreadable processed cheese, such as Dairylea or Kraft

6–8 slices Emmental/Swiss cheese

2 large gherkins/pickles, thinly sliced lengthwise, plus extra to serve

SERVES 2

In a frying pan/skillet, combine the onions with one tablespoon of butter and two tablespoons of vegetable oil. Cook over a medium heat, stirring occasionally, until deep golden brown, about 10 minutes. Season lightly and transfer to a small bowl.

In the same pan/skillet, add another 1 tablespoon oil and heat. When hot but not smoking, add the beef and cook for 2–3 minutes, stirring often until cooked through. Season lightly and set aside.

To assemble, cut the ciabatta in half at the middle to obtain two even pieces, and slice these in half widthways. Spread the inside of the bottom slice of each half with a portion of the processed cheese. With a small brush, coat the outsides of the bread lightly, on both sides, with oil.

Assemble just before cooking, in a large, heavy-based non-stick frying pan/skillet. Depending on the size of your pan/skillet, you may need to cook one sandwich at a time.

Put the plain slices of bread, oil side down, in the pan/skillet. Arrange half the Emmental/Swiss cheese slices on top of these bread slices, then top each bread slice with half the beef and half the onions. Cover with the processed cheese-coated bread slice and place on top of the sandwich to enclose, oil-side up.

Turn the heat to medium and cook the first side for 3–5 minutes until deep golden, pressing gently with a large spatula. Carefully turn with the spatula and cook on the other side, for 2–3 minutes more or until deep golden brown all over.

Remove from the pan and cut in half. Let cool for a few minutes before serving. Repeat for the remaining sandwich if necessary.

PICKLED BEETROOT, GOAT'S CHEESE & CHILLI JAM

A ZINGY COMBINATION OF COLOURS AND TASTES – PERFECT FOR BRUNCH OR A LATE EVENING SNACK. USE AN ORDINARY MOZZARELLA FOR THIS SANDWICH, AS ITS PRESENCE IS MERELY FOR ADDED OOZE AND TO HELP HOLD THE SANDWICH TOGETHER.

4 slices white or brioche bread

Unsalted butter, softened

50 g/1¾ oz. soft goat's cheese

2–4 tablespoons chilli jam, plus extra for serving

6–8 slices pickled beet(root)

Freshly squeezed juice of ½ lemon

1–2 sprigs fresh dill, leaves chopped

125 g/4½ oz. mozzarella, sliced

SERVES 2

Butter each of the slices of bread on one side.

This is easiest if assembled in a large heavy-based non-stick frying pan/skillet. Put two slices of bread in the pan/skillet, butter-side down. If you can only fit one slice in your pan/skillet, you'll need to cook one sandwich at a time. Add half of the goat's cheese to each slice. Top with half of the chilli jam, spread evenly to the edges. Arrange half of the beet(root) slices on top, squeeze over some lemon juice and scatter over half of the dill. Top each slice with half of the mozzarella and cover with another slice of bread, butter-side up.

Turn the heat to medium and cook the first side for 3–5 minutes until deep golden, pressing gently with a spatula. Carefully turn with a large spatula and cook on the second side, for 2–3 minutes more or until deep golden brown all over.

Remove from the pan/skillet, transfer to a plate and cut each sandwich in half. Let cool for a few minutes before serving. Repeat for the remaining sandwich if necessary. Serve with additional chilli jam, for dipping.

ROASTED BUTTERNUT SQUASH, RICOTTA & PARMESAN WITH SAGE BUTTER

THIS SANDWICH HAS A HIDDEN TWIST THANKS TO THE ADDITION OF SAGE-INFUSED BROWN BUTTER. IT IS A VERY SIMPLE COMBINATION THAT RELIES ON THE BEST QUALITY CHEESE FOR SUCCESS, SO DO NOT SKIMP HERE. EXCELLENT PARMESAN IS KEY.

250 g/1½ cups butternut squash pieces, fresh or frozen

Salt and freshly ground black pepper

4 slices white or sourdough bread

Unsalted butter, softened

4 tablespoons ricotta

2 thin slices mild cheese, such as Gouda or Fontina

1 tablespoon vegetable oil

2–3 tablespoons grated/shredded Parmesan

FOR THE SAGE BUTTER

50 g/3 tablespoons unsalted butter

A few sprigs fresh sage, leaves stripped

Squeeze of fresh lemon juice

SERVES 2

Preheat the oven to 200°C (400°F) Gas 6. Coat the butternut squash with the oil and arrange in a single layer on a baking sheet. Season with salt and pepper and roast until tender and golden brown, around 20–30 minutes. Remove from the oven and crush coarsely. Set aside.

Meanwhile, for the sage butter, melt the butter in a small saucepan until gently sizzling and beginning to deepen in colour. Add the sage leaves and remove from the heat as soon as the leaves crisp up. Add the lemon juice and let stand until needed.

Spread softened butter on the outside of the bread slices on one side and spread two of the slices on the non-buttered side with the ricotta, evenly divided.

This is easiest if assembled in a large, heavy-based non-stick frying pan/skillet. Put two slices of bread in the pan/skillet, butter-side down. If you can only fit one slice in your pan/skillet, you'll need to cook one sandwich at a time. Top each of the bread slices with one slice of Gouda or Fontina and some of the crushed butternut squash, spread evenly to the edges. Drizzle over liberal amounts of the sage butter, but no more than half per slice. Sprinkle half of the Parmesan over each slice and cover with the remaining bread slices, ricotta side down.

Turn the heat to medium and cook the first side for 3–5 minutes until deep golden, pressing gently with a spatula. Carefully turn with a spatula and cook on the second side, for 2–3 minutes more or until deep golden brown all over.

Remove from the pan/skillet, transfer to a plate and cut in half diagonally. Let cool for a few minutes before serving. Repeat for the remaining sandwich if necessary. Any remaining sage butter can be drizzled over the sandwiches before serving.

BRAISED CHICORY, BLUE CHEESE, SERRANO HAM & WALNUT PESTO

SALTY, BITTER, SWEET AND NUTTY ALL COLLIDE IN THIS DECADENT, IBERIAN-INSPIRED SANDWICH. IT IS UNUSUAL AS WELL AS ELEGANT SO SERVE AS A DINNER PARTY APPETIZER WITH A GLASS OF CHILLED SPANISH WHITE, OR TRY IT FOR AN OUT OF THE ORDINARY MIDWEEK SUPPER.

1 large chicory/endive, halved and thinly sliced lengthwise

1 tablespoon butter

1 tablespoon vegetable oil

125 ml/½ cup dry white wine

4 slices white bread

Unsalted butter, softened

90 g/3 oz. soft blue cheese, at room temperature

2 thin slices Gouda or Fontina

4–6 slices Serrano ham

FOR THE WALNUT PESTO

100g/1 cup walnut pieces

80 g/1 cup grated/shredded Parmesan

Small bunch of fresh flat-leaf parsley, leaves stripped

1 clove garlic, peeled

About 150 ml/⅔ cup rapeseed oil

Drizzle of honey

Salt and freshly ground black pepper

Juice of ½ lemon, or more to taste

SERVES 2

For the walnut pesto, combine all the ingredients in a food processor and process until it forms a spreadable paste. Taste and add more salt, pepper and lemon juice as required. Set aside.

Combine the chicory/endive slivers, butter and oil in a non-stick frying pan/skillet and cook over a medium heat until soft and beginning to brown. Add the wine, boil for 1 minute, then season, lower the heat, cover and simmer for 5 minutes. Remove the lid and continue cooking gently until the liquid evaporates. Then, coarsely chop the chicory/endive and set aside.

Spread softened butter on each of the bread slices on one side. Spread two of the slices with the blue cheese, evenly divided, on the other side and spread the remaining two slices with pesto on the non-buttered side.

This is easiest if assembled in a large, heavy-based non-stick frying pan/skillet. Put the pesto-covered slices of bread in the pan/skillet, butter-side down. Top each with one slice of cheese, half of the chicory/endive and half of the ham. Finally, top with with the blue cheese bread slices, butter side up.

Turn the heat to medium and cook the first side for 3–5 minutes until deep golden, pressing gently with a spatula. Carefully turn with a large spatula and cook on the other side, for 2–3 minutes more or until deep golden brown all over.

Remove from the pan/skillet and transfer to a plate. Let cool for a few minutes before serving. Repeat for the remaining sandwich if necessary.

NOTE: Leftover pesto can be kept in the refrigerator in a sealed container.

TARTIFLETTE

A FRIED POTATO SANDWICH, LAYERED WITH WINE-INFUSED MELTING ONIONS AND REBLOCHON CHEESE – FOOD DOES NOT GET MUCH BETTER. TO COUNTERACT ALL THE CARBS, SERVE WITH A SALAD OF SLICED LITTLE GEM HEARTS DRIZZLED WITH A TANGY, MUSTARDY VINAIGRETTE. MAYBE FOLLOW WITH A BRISK WALK, OR A NAP, AS MOOD DICTATES!

425 g/15 oz. waxy potatoes, peeled and thinly sliced

1 tablespoon vegetable oil

1 teaspoon salt

1 medium onion, thinly sliced

Knob/pat of butter

1–2 slices pancetta or bacon, finely chopped

½ teaspoon dried thyme

Salt and freshly ground black pepper

4 tablespoons dry white wine

2 tablespoons unsalted butter, melted

1 medium baguette, cut in two lengthways and widthways, or 4 large slices pain au levain

160 g/5½ oz. Reblochon, chilled and thinly sliced

SERVES 2

Preheat the oven to 190°C (375°F) Gas 5.

Generously coat a small baking dish with butter. Arrange the potato slices in the dish, drizzle over some oil and sprinkle with salt. Roast for 20–30 minutes, turning once, until brown around the edges and tender.

Meanwhile, put the onion slices in a small frying pan/skillet with a knob/pat of butter and cook over a medium heat, stirring occasionally, until golden and soft. Add the pancetta and thyme and cook for a few minutes more. Add the wine and cook until evaporated. Season lightly and set aside.

Brush the outsides of the bread with the melted butter. Arrange butter-side down on a clean work surface or chopping board. Arrange half the cheese, potatoes and onions over one slice and repeat with another slice. Finally, top with the remaining bread slices, butter-side up.

Place the sandwiches in a large, heavy-based non-stick frying pan/skillet. Depending on the size of your pan/skillet, you may need to cook one sandwich at a time.

Turn the heat to medium and cook the first side for 3–4 minutes until deep golden, pressing gently with a spatula. Carefully turn with a large spatula and cook on the other side, for 2–3 minutes more or until deep golden brown all over.

Remove from the pan/skillet and allow to cool for a few minutes before serving. Repeat for the remaining sandwich if necessary.

AVOCADO, TOMATO, BABY SPINACH & SMOKED CHICKEN

BRIGHT AND LIGHT, THIS IS A CALIFORNIAN-INSPIRED MIX OF INGREDIENTS FOR A SANDWICH THAT COMES TOGETHER QUICKLY AND EASILY. IDEAL FOR A WEEKEND LUNCH OR BRUNCH, OR EVEN A SIMPLE SUMMER SUPPER.

4 slices granary or wholemeal/whole-wheat bread

Unsalted butter

130 g/1½ cups grated/shredded Red Leicester or mild Cheddar

1 large or 2 small tomatoes, thinly sliced

1 tablespoon balsamic vinegar

Handful fresh baby spinach leaves, washed and dried

175 g/6 oz. smoked chicken, thinly sliced

1 small avocado, coarsely mashed with a fork

SERVES 2

Butter each of the bread slices on one side and arrange buttered-side down on a clean work surface or chopping board.

This is easiest if assembled in a large heavy-based non-stick frying pan/skillet. Put two slices of bread in the pan/skillet, butter-side down. If you can only fit one slice in your pan/skillet, cook one sandwich at a time. Sprinkle each of these slices with half the cheese in an even layer, then add half of the tomato slices and finally half of the balsamic vinegar. Arrange a thin layer of spinach leaves on top, then top this with the chicken.

Spread half of the avocado on the other pieces of bread still on your work surface or chopping board and put them on top of the chicken to enclose, butter-side up. Depending on the size of your pan/skillet, you may need to cook one sandwich at a time.

Turn the heat to medium and cook the first side for 3–4 minutes until deep golden, pressing gently with a spatula. Carefully turn with a large spatula and cook on the other side, for 2–3 minutes more or until deep golden brown all over.

Remove from the pan/skillet and let cool for a few minutes before serving. Repeat for the remaining sandwich if necessary.

MARINATED ARTICHOKE, OLIVE & PROVOLONE

NEXT TIME YOU FEEL THE NEED FOR PIZZA, TRY THIS INSTEAD. MOST OF THE INGREDIENTS ARE PANTRY STAPLES, SO LEAVING THE HOUSE TO MAKE IT MAY NOT EVEN BE NECESSARY. THIS SANDWICH IS SIMPLE TO THROW TOGETHER AND QUICKER THAN A PIZZA TO MAKE – PERFECT WHEN YOU NEED SOMETHING TASTY, IN A HURRY.

Unsalted butter, melted

4 slices panini bread

1–2 tablespoons sun-dried tomato paste

180 g/6 oz Provolone, grated/shredded or thinly sliced

6–8 marinated artichokes, drained and sliced

65 g/½ cup pitted/stoned green olives, coarsely chopped

½ teaspoon dried oregano

SERVES 2

Brush butter on the bread slices on one side. Spread two of the slices with sun-dried tomato paste on the non-buttered side and set aside. Divide the cheese into two equal portions.

Assemble the sandwiches in a large, non-stick griddle pan or a panini grill/press if you have one. Put two slices of bread in the griddle pan, butter-side down. If you can only fit one slice in your pan/skillet, cook one sandwich at a time. Top each slice with half of one of the cheese portions. Arrange half the artichokes on top and sprinkle with half of the olives and oregano. Sprinkle over the remaining half-portion of cheese and cover with another bread slice, tomato side down.

Turn the heat to medium and cook the first side for 3–5 minutes until deep golden, pressing gently with a spatula. Carefully turn with a large spatula and cook on the other side, for 2–3 minutes more or until deep golden brown all over.

Remove from the pan, transfer to a plate and cut into quarters. Let cool for a few minutes before serving. Repeat for the remaining sandwich if necessary.

LOBSTER TAIL, TARRAGON MAYONNAISE & BEAUFORT

HAVING LIVED FOR SO LONG IN FRANCE, I NOW FIND IT DIFFICULT TO FATHOM PAIRING SHELLFISH WITH CHEESE. IT JUST SEEMS WRONG. BUT IF ANY CHEESE WERE ABLE TO PARTNER LOBSTER, LE ROI OF THE SEAFOOD SET, IT WOULD HAVE TO BE BEAUFORT, THE BEST CHEESE IN THE WORLD. ADD TARRAGON-FLECKED MAYONNAISE AND, SUDDENLY, THE IMPOSSIBLE SEEMS POSSIBLE.

2–3 tablespoons mayonnaise

Small handful fresh tarragon leaves, finely chopped

1 teaspoon freshly squeezed lemon juice

Coarse, freshly ground black pepper

4 large slices brioche bread or rolls

About 250 g/9 oz. lobster meat, cooked

250 g/3 cups grated/shredded Beaufort

Unsalted butter, softened

SERVES 2

In a small bowl, combine the mayonnaise, tarragon, lemon juice and a generous pinch of black pepper. Stir well and set aside.

Butter the bread slices on one side and arrange buttered-side down on a clean work surface or a chopping board. Spread two of the non-buttered sides generously with the tarragon mayonnaise.

Assemble just before cooking, in a large, heavy- based non-stick frying pan/skillet. Depending on the size of your pan/skillet, you may need to cook one sandwich at a time; if it is large enough, place two of the bread slices not spread with tarragon mayonnaise in the pan/skillet, buttered-side down. Top each of these slices with half of the cheese, taking care not to let too much fall into the pan/skillet. Top this with half the lobster, arranging in an even layer over all. Finally, enclose with the mayonnaise-coated slices of bread, buttered-side up.

Turn the heat to medium and cook the first side for 3–4 minutes until deep golden, pressing gently with a large spatula. Carefully turn with the spatula and cook on the other side, for 2–3 minutes more or until deep golden brown all over.

Remove from the pan/skillet and let cool for a few minutes before serving. Repeat for the remaining sandwich if necessary.

INDEX

A

ale 24
apple-cranberry sauce 23
artichoke: Marinated Artichoke, Olive & Provolone 61
avocado: Avocado, Refried Bean & Monterey Jack 32
Avocado, Tomato, Baby Spinach & Smoked Chicken 56

B

bacon 46, 57
baguette 57
Balsamic Mushrooms & Fontina 15
BBQ Ham Hock and Mac 'n' Cheese 45
barbecue sauce 45
Basic Grilled Cheese 8
Beaufort 62
beetroot: Halloumi, Falafel & Beetroot with Tahini Sauce 31
black olive paste 19
blue cheese: Braised Chicory, Blue Cheese, Serrano Ham & Walnut Pesto 54
Brie & Apple-cranberry Sauce 23
brioche 62
burger buns 41
Burger Scamorza 41
Butternut Squash, Ricotta & Parmesan with Sage Butter 53

C

Cheddar 8, 11, 12, 20, 24, 32, 38, 44, 45, 58
chicken: Avocado, Tomato, Baby Spinach & Smoked Chicken 56
Chipotle Chicken, Roasted Green Peppers & Queso Fresco 37
Tandoori Chicken & Mango Chutney with Paneer 34
chicory: Braised Chicory, Blue Cheese, Serrano Ham & Walnut Pesto 54
Chilli Bacon Swiss Cheese 46
Chipotle Chicken, Roasted Green Peppers & Queso Fresco

Chorizo, Mini Peppers & Manchego 28
chutney 11
ciabatta 24, 42, 49

E

Emmental 12, 27, 38, 46, 49
endive see chicory

F

falafel: Halloumi, Falafel & Beetroot with Tahini Sauce 31
flatbread 31
focaccia 19
fontina 15, 34, 37, 42, 53, 54
Frankfurter, Sauerkraut & Mustard 38

G

goat's cheese 50
Gouda 8, 34, 37, 53, 54
Gruyère 8, 16

H

Halloumi, Falafel & Beetroot with Tahini Sauce 31
ham 27

J

jalapeños 45

K

Kimchi & Monterey Jack 20
Leek & Gruyère 16

L

Lincolnshire Poacher 12
Lobster Tail, Tarragon Mayonnaise & Beaufort 62

M

Manchego 28
mango: Tandoori Chicken & Mango Chutney with Paneer 34
Marinated Artichoke, Olive & Provolone 61
Monte Cristo 27
Meatballs, Garlic Tomato Sauce & Fontina 42

Monterey Jack 8, 20, 32, 45
mozzarella 12, 19, 41
Mozzarella Puttanesca 19
mushrooms: Balsamic Mushrooms & Fontina 15
mustard: Frankfurter, Sauerkraut & Mustard 38

N

naan bread 34

P

pancetta 57
paneer 34
panini bread 61
Parmesan 19, 53, 54
passata 19
Philly Cheese Steak Sandwich 49
Pickled Beetroot, Goat's Cheese & Chilli Jam 50
pickles 49
potatoes 57
provolone 61
pumpernickel bread 34
Puttanesca, Mozzarella 19

Q

queso fresco 37

R

raita 34
reblochon 57
Red Leicester 58
Red Onion Chutney & Cheddar 11
refried beans 32
ricotta: Butternut Squash, Ricotta & Parmesan with Sage Butter 53
rye bread 38

S

salsa 32
sauerkraut: Frankfurter, Sauerkraut & Mustard 38
sauces: Brie & Apple-Cranberry Sauce 23
Halloumi, Falafel & Beetroot with Tahini Sauce 31
Meatballs, Garlic Tomato Sauce & Fontina 42

scamorza 41
serrano ham: Braised Chicory, Blue Cheese, Serrano Ham & Walnut Pesto 54
sourdough 24, 28, 45
spinach: Avocado, Tomato, Baby Spinach & Smoked Chicken 32
strained tomatoes see passata
strawberry jam/jello 27
sun-dried tomato paste 19
Swiss cheese see Emmental

T

tahini: Halloumi, Falafel & Beetroot with Tahini Sauce 31
Tandoori Chicken and Mango Chutney with Paneer 34
Tartiflette 57
Three Cheese 12

W

walnut bread 23
walnut pesto: Braised Chicory, Blue Cheese, Serrano Ham & Walnut Pesto 54
Welsh Rarebit 24
wine, dry white 54, 57
wine vinegar 15

Y

yogurt 34